A Guide to
AMERICAN STATES

Florida

THE SUNSHINE STATE

MEDIA ENHANCED BOOKS
AV2 BY WEIGL
ADDED VALUE • AUDIO VISUAL

www.av2books.com

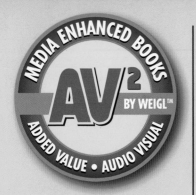

AV[2] provides enriched content that supplements and complements this book. Weigl's AV[2] books strive to create inspired learning and engage young minds in a total learning experience.

Your AV[2] Media Enhanced books come alive with...

Audio
Listen to sections of the book read aloud.

Key Words
Study vocabulary, and complete a matching word activity.

Video
Watch informative video clips.

Quizzes
Test your knowledge.

Go to **www.av2books.com**, and enter this book's unique code.

Embedded Weblinks
Gain additional information for research.

Slide Show
View images and captions, and prepare a presentation.

BOOK CODE

U11508

AV[2] **by Weigl** brings you media enhanced books that support active learning.

Try This!
Complete activities and hands-on experiments.

... and much, much more!

Published by AV[2] by Weigl
350 5th Avenue, 59th Floor
New York, NY 10118
Website: www.av2books.com   www.weigl.com

Copyright 2012 AV[2] by Weigl
All rights reserved. No part of this publication may be reproduced, stored in a retrieval system, or transmitted in any form or by any means, electronic, mechanical, photocopying, recording, or otherwise, without the prior written permission of the publisher.

Library of Congress Cataloging-in-Publication Data

Sullivan, Ann, 1966-
 Florida / Ann Sullivan.
    p. cm. -- (A guide to American states)
Includes index.
 ISBN 978-1-61690-781-5 (hardcover : alk. paper) -- ISBN 978-1-61690-457-9 (online)
1. Florida--Juvenile literature. I. Title.
 F311.3.S853 2011
 975.9--dc23
                          2011018320

Printed in the United States of America in North Mankato, Minnesota

052011
WEP180511

Project Coordinator Jordan McGill
Art Director Terry Paulhus

Photo Credits
Every reasonable effort has been made to trace ownership and to obtain permission to reprint copyright material. The publishers would be pleased to have any errors or omissions brought to their attention so that they may be corrected in subsequent printings.

Weigl acknowledges Getty Images as its primary image supplier for this title.

Contents

Florida's many beautiful lakes attract tourists, who boat, fish, swim, and water-ski.

Introduction

Millions of people know Florida as a great place to vacation. Many people have come to marvel at Walt Disney World and Sea World or to learn about the past, present, and future of space exploration at the Kennedy Space Center in Cape Canaveral. Others dive in to explore the ocean's colorful coral reefs or watery wrecks of ships that sank long ago.

But Florida is much more than that. This southeastern state produces the most **citrus** fruit of any state in the United States. Florida also produces dairy and beef goods and manufactures forest products.

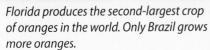
Florida produces the second-largest crop of oranges in the world. Only Brazil grows more oranges.

Killer whales entertain thousands every year at Sea World.

Throughout the winter months, Florida grows fruit and vegetable crops. These foods, along with Florida's famous orange juice, end up in homes across the United States and in other countries.

Northern and southern Florida are very different. Northern Florida is more rural, hillier, and colder than southern Florida. Much of its economy is based on farming and forestry. It also has older settlements than southern Florida, which is warmer, flatter, and more recently settled. Southern Florida's economy is based on tourism, citrus fruits, vegetables, and livestock.

Where Is Florida?

For most Americans, a trip to Florida means heading south or southeast, perhaps for thousands of miles. Except for Hawai'i, Florida is the southernmost state in the country. Georgia and Alabama border Florida to the north, Alabama borders Florida to the west, and water surrounds the rest of the state. Most of Florida is a long **peninsula**, with the Atlantic Ocean on one side and the Gulf of Mexico on the other. This peninsula stretches hundreds of miles from Jacksonville in the north to below Miami in the south. At the end of the peninsula lies the Florida Keys, a string of islands trailing off into the Gulf of Mexico.

Built in the 1930s, Miami Beach's Historic District showcases buildings in a style known as Miami Beach Art Deco.

The great climate attracts many tourists and retirees escaping cold winter weather farther north. It also attracts people who want to stay year-round. Florida is one of the fastest-growing states in the United States and the fourth most populous in the country. Thousands of people have moved to the state from countries in the Caribbean, including Cuba and Haiti. Miami–Dade County, which includes the cities of Miami, Hialeah, and Miami Beach, is the most populous of the 67 counties in Florida.

Along with the climate, water plays a huge role in drawing people to Florida. Natural springs gush with freshwater. There are more than 7,700 lakes in the state, and **wetlands** such as the Everglades and the Big Cypress Swamp cover large areas.

Bald cypress trees thrive in wetlands and along the shores of lakes.

I DIDN'T KNOW THAT!

Spain sold the land that is now Florida to the United States in 1819.

Florida's first state flag had a ribbon with the inscription "Let us alone." It flew from 1845 to 1861.

Tallahassee, the capital city, was chosen in 1824 because it was halfway between St. Augustine and Pensacola. The new location meant the government no longer had to make the 20-day trip by horse between St. Augustine and Pensacola for alternating sessions.

Florida became a popular resort area more than 100 years ago.

The panther is a large, long-tailed cat. It lives in forests and the Everglades, much the same as whitetailed deer. Deer are one of the cat's main foods.

Florida's state reptile is the alligator, state fish is the largemouth bass, and state shell is the conch.

Mapping Florida

From the St. Marys River in the north to the tip of the Florida Keys, Florida is 447 miles long. It is 361 miles wide across the northern panhandle, a strip of land that juts out from the larger area of Florida. The panhandle stretches from the Atlantic Ocean on the east to the Perdido River on the west. The greatest width of the Florida peninsula is 150 miles.

Sites and Symbols

STATE SEAL
Florida

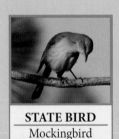

STATE BIRD
Mockingbird

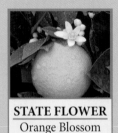

STATE FLOWER
Orange Blossom

STATE FLAG
Florida

STATE ANIMAL
Florida panther

STATE TREE
Sabal Palm

Nickname The Sunshine State

Motto In God We Trust

Song "Old Folks at Home" words by and music by Stephen C. Foster

Entered the Union March 3, 1845, as the 27th state

Capital Tallahassee

Population (2010 Census) 18,801,310

Ranked 4th state

ALABAMA

GEORGIA

Tifton
Douglas
Moultrie
Waycross
Brunswick

Dothan
Brewton
Graceville
Marianna
Thomasville
Valdosta
Folkston

Fernandina Beach

Niceville
Pensacola
Killearn
Madison
Jasper

Tallahassee
Perry
Lake City
Lakeside
Jacksonville
Jacksonville Beach

Panama City
Port St. Joe
High Springs
Starke
St. Augustine

Apalachicola
Cross City
Gainesville
Palm Coast

Williston
Ocala
Daytona Beach

De Land

Crystal River
Leesburg

Brooksville
Orlando

Cocoa
Cocoa Beach

Land O Lakes
Kissimmee
Melbourne

Clearwater
Tampa
Winter Haven

Largo

FLORIDA
Vero Beach

St. Petersburg
Wauchula
Avon Park

Bradenton
Fort Pierce

Sarasota
Okeechobee

Venice

Port Charlotte
West Palm Beach

Fort Myers

Immokalee
Pompano Beach

Golden Gate
Fort Lauderdale

Naples
Hollywood

Hialeah

Kendall
Miami

Homestead

Key Largo

ATLANTIC OCEAN

GULF

OF

MEXICO

N

Map Scale

0   100 Miles

LEGEND
— Road
— River
⭐ State Capital
• City
▢ Florida
— State Border

STATE CAPITAL

Tallahassee is well-known for being the only Confederate capital east of the Mississippi River that was not captured during the Civil War. Because of this, many of its older buildings were preserved, including beautiful **plantation** houses and the Old Capitol building. In fact, Tallahassee has two capitol buildings, the old one built in 1842 and the New Capitol building, completed in 1977. The Old Capitol building then became the Museum of Florida History.

United States

Hawai'i   **Alaska**

Florida

The Land

U ntil about 25 million years ago, the Gulf of Mexico and the Atlantic Ocean connected through the center of Florida. Over millions of years, layers of sand and **fossilized** shells built up in the water, creating flat, marshy land. Humans have also changed the landscape by draining marshes, filling in bays, and cutting down forests.

Florida's physical geography is divided into several basic areas. They are the coastal lowlands including the Lake Okeechobee–Everglades basin and Kissimmee lowlands, the Marianna lowlands, the central highlands, the Tallahassee hills, and the western highlands. Much of Florida is quite flat. The highest point is in Walton County, just 345 feet above sea level.

FLORIDA PANHANDLE

Short, bushlike palm trees called palmettos, as well as grasses, grow on the sand dunes in the Florida Panhandle.

COASTAL LOWLANDS

Coral reefs off the coastal lowlands shelter many kinds of fish.

LAKE OKEECHOBEE-EVERGLADES BASIN

The Lake Okeechobee-Everglades basin is actually a shallow slow-moving river. Okeechobee means "river of grass."

FLORIDA KEYS

Made of coral and limestone, the Florida Keys extend over 200 miles from Virginia Key to Loggerhead Key.

In the winter, southern Florida is one of the warmest places in the nation.

Climate

Florida's southern location gives it long, hot summers and short, mild winters. Heavy rainfall often occurs between April and November. The hurricane season lasts from June to November, though hurricanes are most likely to happen in September. The average temperature ranges from 68° Fahrenheit in the north in Tallahassee to 77° F in Florida's southern tip, Key West.

The hottest day ever recorded in Florida was June 29, 1931, when the temperature rose to 109° F in Monticello. The coldest temperature recorded was –2° F in Tallahassee in 1899. Several cities in the panhandle reported snow that day as well.

Average Annual Precipitation Across Florida

Cities in different parts of Florida typically receive different amounts of rainfall over the course of a year. What might be one reason Walt Disney chose to build Walt Disney World in the Orlando area?

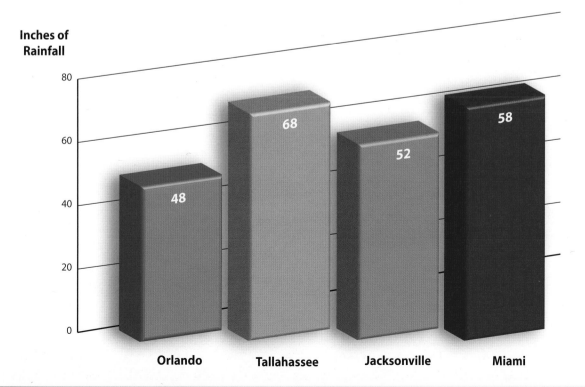

Natural Resources

Florida has an important **phosphate** mining industry. Deposits are usually found 15 to 30 feet below Earth's surface. Early miners used picks and shovels to mine phosphate. Electricity and machines have made mining easier, allowing workers to mine large areas. Thousands of acres are now mined, producing millions of tons of phosphate annually.

Florida produces about three-fourths of the country's phosphate and one-fourth of the world's supply. Phosphate is important to farmers because it is used to make fertilizer.

Slash pines form an important part of the lumber industry. Their strong, heavy wood is used in construction.

Trees are another important natural resource. A little less than half of Florida is covered with forests, and there are more kinds of trees here than anywhere else in the United States except Hawai'i. Pine is the main **commercial** tree. It is used to make paper and other related products. Most tree farming happens in northern Florida, but some forestland is also found in the southwestern region of the state.

Fish and other marine animals are another major resource. Florida ranks high among the states for the amount of seafood it produces. Commercial fishers sell their catches to restaurants and factories.

Plants

Colorful plants such as orchids, lilies, and purple morning glory grow in different **habitats**. Mangrove trees grow well in warm, salty water along the coast. Cypress trees also live in wet areas. Forests of pine, beech, and magnolia trees cover almost half of the state and are the home of deer, foxes, and wild cats, including the Florida panther. The northern area supports hardwoods, loblolly pines, and longleaf pines as well as oak trees and saw palmettos. Saw grass, cypress, sabal palm, myrtle, willow, elderberry, and gum thrive in the Lake Okeechobee–Everglades basin.

SAW GRASS

Saw grass has spiny, toothed leaf blades that resemble a saw. Birds eat its seeds, and animals build nests from its leaves.

ORANGE TREE

Orange trees can bear fruit for between 40 and 80 years. Oranges provide vitamin C and some vitamin A.

GUMBO-LIMBO TREE

The gumbo-limbo is often called the "tourist tree." The tree's reddish bark peels, like the skin of tourists with sunburn.

RED MANGROVE TREE

The roots of the red mangrove tree filter the salt from seawater. They also anchor eroding land.

Citrus trees are native to Southeast Asia, and cultivation of lemon, lime, and orange trees began there before 4000 BC. These trees have been grown in Florida for more than 400 years.

More than 300 different kinds of trees grow in Florida.

Florida's state wildflower is the coreopsis. Highways and roads have been planted with this beautiful flower, which ranges in color from gold to pink.

Most of the fresh strawberries eaten in the winter in the United States are grown on the 8,300 acres of farmland surrounding Plant City.

Animals

Florida's heat and unique environment make it home to plants and animals that are not found anywhere else in the country. However, the best-known animals in the state are alligators and crocodiles. A wide variety of living things, from tiny dragonflies to giant sea turtles, also live in Florida. Flamingos, ibis, and herons wade in warm, marshy areas along the coast. Warm temperatures also attract thousands of **migratory** birds that fly south for the winter.

The Everglades and the Big Cypress Swamp are huge wetland areas in southwestern Florida, where thousands of animals, plants, and birds live. The Everglades are the only place in the world where alligators and crocodiles, which look very much alike, live side by side. More than two dozen kinds of snakes, only four of them poisonous, live in the Everglades, too. Colorful insects, including the lubber grasshopper and the sulfur butterfly, are also found there.

LEATHERBACK SEA TURTLE

Female sea turtles come to shore to lay their leathery eggs in the warm sand. The temperature of the sand controls whether the baby turtles will be male or female.

LARGEMOUTH BASS

Florida's state fish is the largemouth bass. These fish prefer to swim in areas that contain logs, debris, and weeds.

LUBBER GRASSHOPPER

Lubber grasshoppers have sharp spikes on their hind legs to protect them from possible predators. They also contain poison, which may cause predators to vomit.

DUSKY PYGMY RATTLESNAKE

The dusky pygmy rattlesnake is one of the few poisonous snakes in Florida. It lives in pine forests and prairies, near lakes and ponds, and along the edge of marshes and cypress swamps.

Loss of habitat contributed to the decline of Florida alligator populations in the 1950s and 1960s. The population has recovered after the alligator was put on the **endangered species** list in 1967.

Flamingos are pink because of natural chemicals in the shrimps and other foods that they eat.

Fish, shellfish, birds, and other wildlife feed and raise their young among the roots of mangrove trees.

Sea turtles may travel hundreds or thousands of miles to feed and nest. These animals can live 60 years or more.

More than 80 kinds of land animals and 400 kinds of birds live in Florida.

Humans are responsible for much of the manatee's destruction. This endangered species frequently dies as a result of colliding with boats, pollution, and getting caught in fishing lines.

Tourism

Beaches and sunshine draw millions of tourists to Florida each year. Some people want to escape the cold at home, while others come for the amusement parks, the fishing, and the many natural areas that Florida offers.

Walt Disney World is the most famous tourist attraction in Florida and one of the biggest attractions in the world. Other parks in and around Orlando invite visitors to experience the magic of Hollywood filmmaking or watch dolphins and killer whales play in the water.

More than 1 million people visit Everglades National Park every year. The park is the largest remaining **subtropical** wilderness in the continental United States. Within its 1,508,000 acres are freshwater and saltwater areas, tropical hardwood forests, offshore coral reefs, and a wide variety of plants and animals.

EVERGLADES NATIONAL PARK

This national park is the largest subtropical wilderness left in the United States. It includes freshwater and marine habitats and a wide variety of animals, including crocodiles.

WALT DISNEY WORLD

Walt Disney World attracts visitors with its fantastic rides and dazzling parades and shows.

JOHN F. KENNEDY SPACE CENTER

Every U.S. astronaut has taken off from the Kennedy Space Center in Cape Canaveral. Visitors can view old rockets and other space-exploration equipment, talk with astronauts, and learn about unpiloted probes to other planets.

THE WIZARDING WORLD OF HARRY POTTER

Fans flock to the Wizarding World of Harry Potter, a Universal Orlando attraction that opened in 2010. They can tour Hogwarts Castle, explore the streets of Hogsmeade village, and go on fabulous rides.

Industry

ourism has always been an important industry in Florida. During the 1870s, business leaders such as Henry Flagler and Henry B. Plant began building railroads to link Florida to the North. They also had hotels constructed close to their railroad lines to accommodate tourists. In fact, Flagler built the Ponce de Leon, Florida's first magnificent tourist hotel.

Industries in Florida
Value of Goods and Services in Millions of Dollars

The pie chart below shows how important certain industries are to Florida. Since the 1970s, Florida has had one of the fastest-growing economies in the United States. Tourism has been a major cause of that growth. What industries help meet the needs of tourists and thrive because of tourism?

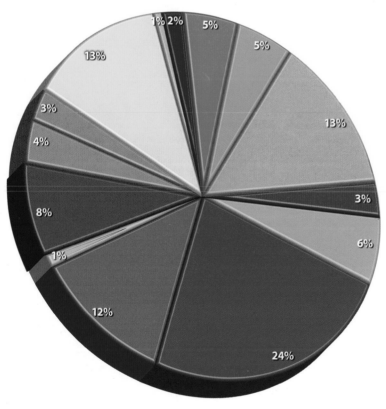

LEGEND

	Industry	Value
	Agriculture, Forestry, and Fishing	$5,476
*	Mining	$1,188
	Utilities	$16,353
	Construction	$39,555
	Manufacturing	$36,122
	Wholesale and Retail Trade	$99,491
	Transportation	$20,385
	Media and Entertainment	$43,554
	Finance, Insurance, and Real Estate	$177,326
	Professional and Technical Services	$87,925
	Education	$6,741
	Health Care	$57,599
	Hotels and Restaurants	$30,195
	Other Services	$20,720
	Government	$94,406

TOTAL $737,036

*Less than 1%. Percentages may not add to 100 because of rounding.

Tourism is now the largest industry in Florida. It has created the need for smaller industries, such as wine making.

Farming is another important industry, but it does not employ huge numbers of people. Florida farmers grow fruits and vegetables, including most of the nation's orange and other citrus crops. Many of these crops are processed, or modified to be used in other products.

Tomatoes are a major crop for farmers in Florida.

Goods and Services

Most people would have no trouble naming one of the most important goods produced in Florida. Oranges are probably the first thing people think of. Whether oranges are fresh, squeezed into juice, or made into other products, they provide a huge source of income for Florida farmers.

Other citrus crops grown in Florida include grapefruits, lemons, limes, and tangerines. In fact, during the 2009 to 2010 growing season, Florida farmers harvested 159 million boxes of oranges and grapefruits. Harvest season may start as early as August for some kinds of fruit, and it continues until June.

Over the next 20 years, researchers predict there will be a growing number of jobs in Florida for health-care providers such as nurses.

During the winter, when other parts of the country cannot grow food because of cold weather, Florida workers harvest tomatoes, potatoes, celery, carrots, lettuce, and other crops. Some farmers raise Thoroughbred horses. Others raise beef or dairy cattle, chickens, or hogs. Some people make their living by fishing for crab, lobster, or shrimps.

More people in Florida work in service jobs than in any other type of job, which means they help other people and businesses. Service workers include people who work in amusement parks, stores, and other tourist attractions. Health-care workers, park rangers, teachers, police officers, firefighters, and other government workers all provide services as well.

The Spanish brought cattle to Florida in the 1500s. The Seminole tribe has been raising them ever since.

American Indians

American Indians were the first people to live in Florida. Scientists say they came to Florida more than 10,000 years ago. They were nomadic hunters, which means they followed the animals they hunted and did not live in permanent settlements. They hunted with stone-tipped arrows and spears. Over hundreds of years, they started to live in villages, fishing during winter months and growing crops such as corn.

Seminoles still build traditional houses, called **chickees**, *in the Everglades.*

At least four major tribes lived in Florida, including the Calusa, the Tequesta, the Timucua, and the Apalachee. By 1750, most of these tribes had been destroyed by diseases brought by settlers, by traders taking Indians as slaves, and by war. During the 1700s, Seminole Indians arrived from farther north.

By the early 1800s, settlers wanted to take over the land and move the American Indians west of the Mississippi River. This led to the Seminole Wars. Many people died in the wars, and thousands of American Indians were sent to live outside Florida. The descendants of the American Indians who survived in Florida are members of today's Seminole tribe and Miccosukee tribe. Both of these groups have succeeded in keeping their language and culture alive.

In traditional Seminole communities, the women farmed, raised the children, and owned the household, the fields, and all their crops.

The three Seminole Wars were fought between 1814 and 1858. By the late 1800s, the remaining American Indians and settlers in Florida had begun to trade peacefully.

Osceola led the American Indian warriors and fought to remain in Florida when Indians were being sent west. In 1837, a U.S. army commander asked Osceola and some of his men to meet for a peace discussion. The commander then seized Osceola and put him in prison, where he died several months later.

The Seminole of Florida call themselves the Unconquered People. They are descended from just 300 Seminoles who avoided capture by U.S. troops during the 1800s.

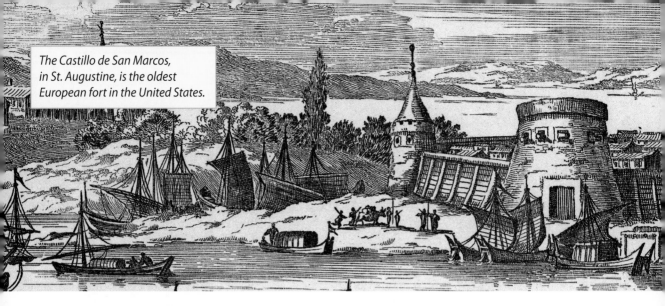

The Castillo de San Marcos, in St. Augustine, is the oldest European fort in the United States.

Explorers and Missionaries

C lose to Easter in 1513, Juan Ponce de León sailed to the northeastern coast of Florida. The Spanish explorer landed near what is now St. Augustine and declared the land *Pascua Florida*, which means "feast of flowers," a name for Easter in Spanish.

Other Spanish explorers eager to find gold and glory in Florida followed Ponce de León. Pánfilo de Narváez and Álvar Núñez Cabeza de Vaca sailed there in 1528. They believed they would find rich American Indian villages, but they found only farming villages.

Other explorers, including Hernando de Soto and Tristan de Luna, sailed to Florida from Cuba and Mexico in the 1500s. None of them succeeded in setting up a permanent colony. In 1565, Pedro Menéndez de Avilés built the first Spanish settlement in Florida, St. Augustine.

Missionaries who wanted to bring their religious message to the American Indians of Florida also arrived in the area. British troops were always a threat, however. They attacked and destroyed Catholic missions, and Spain could not rebuild them.

Timeline of Settlement

Early Exploration

1513 Juan Ponce de León of Spain arrives in Florida.

1564 Frenchman René Goulaine de Laudonnière establishes Fort Caroline along the St. Johns River, near present-day Jacksonville.

1564 Pedro Menéndez de Avilés destroys Fort Caroline and kills most of the people living there.

Early European Settlements

1565 Founded by the Spanish, St. Augustine becomes the first permanent European settlement in the area that is now the United States.

1573 Spanish missionaries come to Florida to spread Christianity. They build churches and missions in southern Florida.

1586 British sea captain and pirate Sir Francis Drake burns St. Augustine.

1763 Spain gives control of Florida to Great Britain.

1784 Spain gains control of Florida from Britain. Spanish settlers and American settlers from the North pour into Florida.

Florida Joins the United States

1819 Spain gives the United States legal title to Florida.

1835–1842 The Second Seminole War results in the U.S. government moving most American Indians in Florida to reservations in Oklahoma.

1840s English-speaking settlers begin settling in Polk and Osceola counties.

Statehood and Civil War

1845 Florida becomes the 27th state.

1861 Florida secedes from the Union. It is readmitted as a state in 1868.

Early Settlers

I n the early 1800s, Florida was mostly wilderness, with a few settlements of American Indians, African Americans, Spanish settlers, and settlers from the United States. Some of the African Americans were escaped slaves from U.S. states in the South. Many people raised cattle or grew crops.

Map of Settlements and Resources in Early Florida

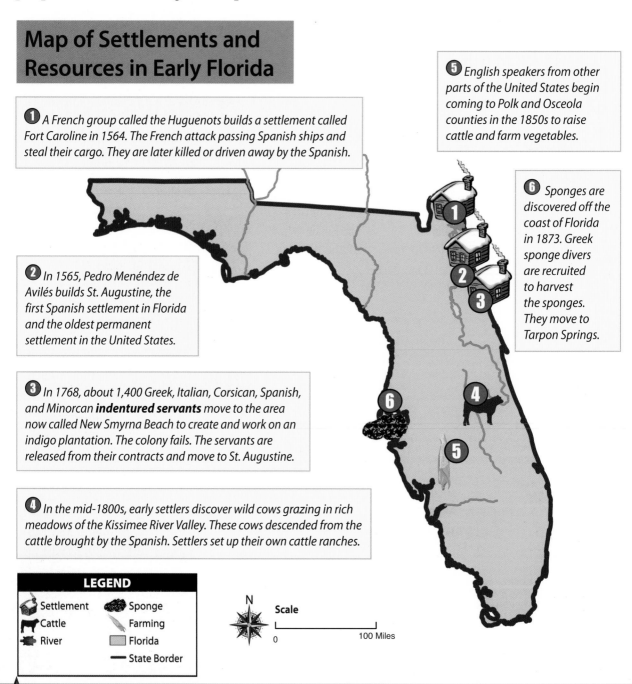

① A French group called the Huguenots builds a settlement called Fort Caroline in 1564. The French attack passing Spanish ships and steal their cargo. They are later killed or driven away by the Spanish.

⑤ English speakers from other parts of the United States begin coming to Polk and Osceola counties in the 1850s to raise cattle and farm vegetables.

⑥ Sponges are discovered off the coast of Florida in 1873. Greek sponge divers are recruited to harvest the sponges. They move to Tarpon Springs.

② In 1565, Pedro Menéndez de Avilés builds St. Augustine, the first Spanish settlement in Florida and the oldest permanent settlement in the United States.

③ In 1768, about 1,400 Greek, Italian, Corsican, Spanish, and Minorcan **indentured servants** move to the area now called New Smyrna Beach to create and work on an indigo plantation. The colony fails. The servants are released from their contracts and move to St. Augustine.

④ In the mid-1800s, early settlers discover wild cows grazing in rich meadows of the Kissimee River Valley. These cows descended from the cattle brought by the Spanish. Settlers set up their own cattle ranches.

LEGEND

- Settlement
- Cattle
- River
- Sponge
- Farming
- Florida
- State Border

N

Scale

0   100 Miles

Some white settlers ran plantations where they relied on slave labor to grow and harvest crops. Poorer settlers survived by growing and making everything they needed.

People who lived in Florida's towns often worked in the lumber and cotton industries or in government. Industries such as mining led to the development of a railway system. After Florida became a state, the growth of railroads linked major towns in Florida and connected Florida with the rest of the country. This allowed more people to visit the state.

By the early 1900s, Florida was growing quickly. Families settled in areas where swamps had been drained to create farmland. Others bought land in dry areas where canals had been built to supply water.

The development of the plantation system, which depended on slavery, led to an increase in the black population of Florida.

Early settlers thought the Everglade area was useless ground. During the early 1900s, they drained the area to make more farmland.

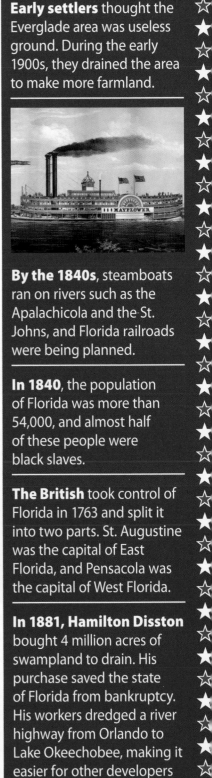

By the 1840s, steamboats ran on rivers such as the Apalachicola and the St. Johns, and Florida railroads were being planned.

In 1840, the population of Florida was more than 54,000, and almost half of these people were black slaves.

The British took control of Florida in 1763 and split it into two parts. St. Augustine was the capital of East Florida, and Pensacola was the capital of West Florida.

In 1881, Hamilton Disston bought 4 million acres of swampland to drain. His purchase saved the state of Florida from bankruptcy. His workers dredged a river highway from Orlando to Lake Okeechobee, making it easier for other developers to get to Florida's interior.

Notable People

Many notable Floridians contributed to the development of their state and their country. They helped protect their peoples and preserve their cultures. Some Floridians served their nation abroad and their fellow workers at home. Others tried to get fair pay and working conditions for union members or to enforce equal rights laws for everyone.

OSCEOLA
(1804–1838)

A brilliant military leader, Osceloa helped the Seminole both fight and hide from the U.S. Army and Florida militia during the Second Seminole War (1835–1842). Although the son of a mixed-blood Creek and probably a Scottish trader, Osceola considered himself fully an Indian. When the U.S. government tried to move the Seminoles to Oklahoma, Osceola and his people hid in the swamps, making use of their knowledge of the land.

GENERAL JOSEPH STILWELL
(1883–1946)

A four-star general, Stilwell was best known for his service in China and Burma before and during World War II. He worked to keep China active in the war against Japan, during a time when China was being run by three separate political groups. Because he disliked formality, was concerned for the soldiers under his command, and had a sharp manner, he earned the nicknames "Uncle Joe" and "Vinegar Joe."

ASA PHILIP RANDOLPH (1889–1979)

A. Philip Randolph organized the first union of African American workers, the Brotherhood of Sleeping Car Porters. Pullman porters worked on railroad cars serving the passengers. They were paid poorly and worked long hours. Despite threats of violence, Randolph gained better pay and working conditions for the union members.

ZORA NEALE HURSTON (1891–1960)

One of eight children, Zora Neale Hurston was born in Eatonville. Soon after her mother died, she left home at age 14. From the 1930s through the 1960s, she wrote plays, musicals, short stories, and novels and collected folklore and folk songs. Her most famous book is *Their Eyes Were Watching God*.

JACQUELINE COCHRAN (c.1906–1980)

When she died in 1980, Cochran held more speed, altitude, and distance records than any other pilot in aviation history. During World War II, she organized civilian women pilots to work for the U.S. military. They flew planes from one airfield to another so that male pilots could be used in the war effort. In 1953 she became the first woman to break the sound barrier.

I DIDN'T KNOW THAT!

Walter Elias Disney (1901–1966) transformed the sleepy little town of Orlando with his vision of an amusement park for all ages. Disney and his brother started buying 28,000 acres in the middle of Florida. Walt Disney World now includes four theme parks, bringing millions of tourists from around the world.

Janet Reno (1938–) was one of only 16 women in a class of more than 500 students in 1960 at Harvard Law School. In 1978, she was elected Florida's State Attorney. As U.S. Attorney General, she focused on enforcing civil rights laws for all Americans, using laws to reduce pollution, and preventing child involvement in gangs, drugs, and violence.

Population

A warm climate, beautiful scenery, and endless outdoor recreation bring more people to the Sunshine State every year. People come from all over the United States and from many other countries to settle in Florida. Most of them live in and around large cities along the coasts, where they enjoy the weather and the recreational activities that Florida offers.

Florida Population 1950–2010

In terms of population, Florida is one of the fastest growing states. What are some of the reasons for this rapid growth?

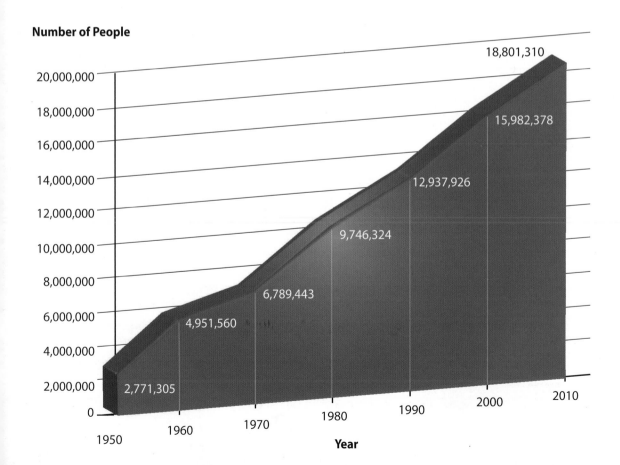

Number of People

- 2,771,305
- 4,951,560
- 6,789,443
- 9,746,324
- 12,937,926
- 15,982,378
- 18,801,310

Year

Florida has more golf courses than any other state and weather that allows golfers to play year–round.

Soldiers who had trained at military bases in Florida during World War II returned with their families to live in Florida after the war.

More than 50 percent of Miami–Dade County's residents were born outside of the United Sates.

Florida is the fourth most populated state, after California, Texas, and New York.

Many retired people live in Florida, giving the state a high proportion of older residents. According to Census Bureau estimates, nearly 80 percent of the population is white, 16 percent is African American, and the remainder come from other backgrounds, such as American Indian and Asian, or claim two or more races. More than 20 percent of Floridians are of Hispanic origin. They or their ancestors are from Spanish-speaking countries, including Cuba, El Salvador, Colombia, and Venezuela.

The week-long Calle Ocho street festival takes place every March in Miami, celebrating all things Latin, including food, music, and dancing.

Politics and Government

Florida joined the Union as the 27th state in 1845. Like other states in the South, Florida supported slavery and state's rights against the policies of the federal government. On January 10, 1861, Florida voted to secede, or withdraw, from the Union. It joined with 10 other Southern states in the Confederate States of America.

Men and boys made up the Confederate volunteers at Warrington Navy Yard in Pensacola, Florida. They had no standard uniforms.

About 15,000 soldiers from Florida (out of a white population of some 70,000) fought for the South during the Civil War. The Confederacy was defeated in 1865. Florida rejoined the Union as a state in 1868 when it finally ratified the 14th Amendment to the U.S. Constitution, which guaranteed civil rights for African Americans.

Today government in Florida centers on the state capital, Tallahassee. Florida's state government has three branches. The executive branch is headed by the governor, who enforces state laws. The legislative branch passes new laws. The legislature has two chambers, the Senate with 40 members and the House of Representatives with 120 members. The judicial branch includes the Florida Supreme Court and lower courts.

The Old Capitol is part of the Capitol Complex in Tallahassee. The current, 72-story Capitol stands nearby.

Cultural Groups

Many different cultural groups have made Florida what it is today: American Indians, people of Spanish, French, and English heritage, African Americans, Cubans, Haitians, and others. Their traditions, foods, music, and beliefs continue to shape Florida's culture.

When European settlers first arrived from Spain, an estimated 350,000 American Indians lived in what is now Florida. Many Indians were wiped out by war, disease, and the slave trade. Others were sent to live in states farther west. Today, more than 2,000 Seminole live on six reservations in the state. They proudly speak two languages, and they share their culture through their art, colorful clothing, and traditions such as basket weaving. Every spring, the Seminole hold a Green Corn Dance, which is a spiritual event to give thanks. The gathering includes many hours of traditional stomp dancing.

About 1 million Cuban Americans live in Florida, many of them immigrants or the descendants of immigrants who arrived between the late 1950s and 1980. With strong attachments to Cuba, they still celebrate changes in the government of that island nation.

Cuban salsa music is popular in Miami and throughout the United States.

About 600 people from the Miccosukee tribe live in Florida today. Many have kept their language, traditional medicine, and traditional clans. Some Miccosukee live in chickees, which are houses made from thatched palmetto over a log frame. Like the Seminole, they celebrate a Green Corn Dance every year.

Over the past 50 years, Hispanic people, many of them immigrants from Cuba and Central America, have had a big influence on Florida culture. About 4 million Hispanic people now call Florida home. They have brought with them their Spanish language, music, and foods, such as black beans, Cuban bread, and café con leche. Annual festivals, including the Cuban American Heritage Festival in Key West, celebrate Spanish culture. Miami and Hialeah both have large Hispanic populations. In some areas, billboards and signs are written only in Spanish. These areas are major centers for Latin American banking, trade, and culture.

I DIDN'T KNOW THAT!

Before the Civil War, African American slaves were not allowed to keep African customs, speak African languages, or practice African religions.

In 1980, more than 120,000 Cuban **refugees** came to the United States during the Mariel Boatlift. Most of them entered through Florida.

Every year, early settlers in St. Augustine held a Posey Dance, based on a Spanish tradition. Single girls attracted dates by placing lit candles in their windows.

The colorful clothing that many Seminole wear is not based on traditional clothing. The Seminole adopted this style of dress in the 1920s.

Arts and Entertainment

What do *Tarzan* and the *Creature from the Black Lagoon* have in common? These films were shot in Florida. Florida's film industry has been strong for more than 100 years. The climate and variety of natural areas in the state attracted early filmmakers looking for jungle settings or mysterious tropical islands. In the early 1900s, Jacksonville was a kind of "Hollywood East." It boasted more than 30 film studios and 1,000 actors and **extras**. The booming industry eventually moved most of its work to Hollywood, but new studios have recently replaced them. For example, both Universal and Disney opened studios in Florida.

A science-fiction classic, Creature from the Black Lagoon *required two different men in two different costumes to play the monster.*

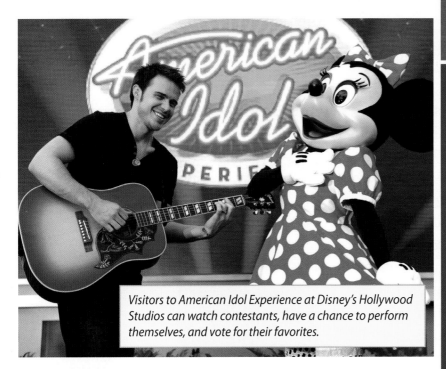

Visitors to American Idol Experience at Disney's Hollywood Studios can watch contestants, have a chance to perform themselves, and vote for their favorites.

Walt Disney World has provided large-scale entertainment to both tourists and local people since 1971. The vast amusement park features music and shows. Visitors to Disney's Hollywood Studios can get a behind-the-scenes look at television shows and filmmaking.

Besides filmmaking, Florida has a wealth of music and theater. The New World Symphony in Miami Beach trains some of the top classical musicians in the country. Hundreds of graduates have gone on to perform with professional orchestras and music groups. Florida has a number of orchestras, including the Florida Orchestra, the Florida Philharmonic Orchestra, and the Jacksonville Symphony.

Florida's Hispanic residents have introduced other kinds of music, such as salsa and Latin jazz. This music is especially popular in southern Florida, where many people of Cuban and Central American origin live. There is also no shortage of theater in Florida, including the Gainesville Community Playhouse.

Sports

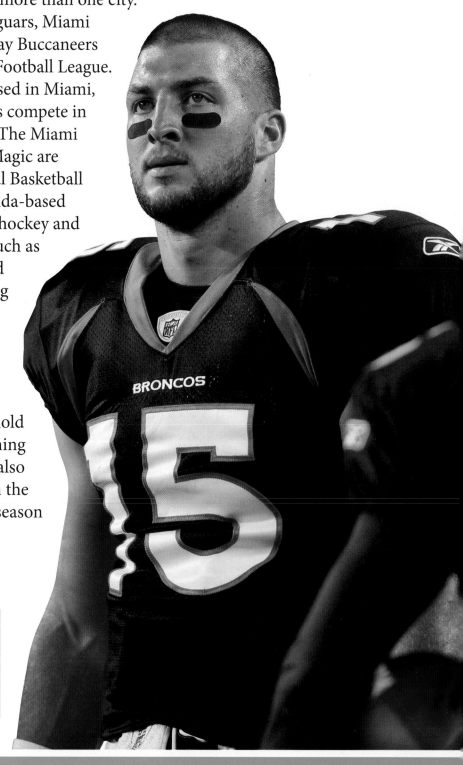

Just about every professional sport is represented in Florida, often in more than one city. The Jacksonville Jaguars, Miami Dolphins, and Tampa Bay Buccaneers all play in the National Football League. The Florida Marlins, based in Miami, and the Tampa Bay Rays compete in Major League Baseball. The Miami Heat and the Orlando Magic are members of the National Basketball Association. Other Florida-based professional teams play hockey and soccer. Some of them, such as the Florida Panthers and the Tampa Bay Lightning of the National Hockey League, were formed only in the 1990s.

About half of the Major League Baseball teams hold their annual spring training camps in Florida. They also play exhibition games in the state before the regular season starts in April.

Tim Tebow led the University of Florida to a national football championship and started his professional career as quarterback with the Denver Broncos.

One of the most talented players in the National Basketball Association, Lebron James plays for the Miami Heat.

Florida high schools and colleges compete in all kinds of sports throughout the year. Florida State University, the University of Florida in Gainesville, and the University of Miami football teams won nine national championships between 1983 and 2010.

Jai alai, pronounced "high lie," is a sport that started in Spain hundreds of years ago. It is popular in Florida, especially in the Miami area. The handball-like game is played with a hard rubber ball, called a pelota, on a three-walled court, called a fronton. Players throw the ball with a wicker basket, called a cesta, attached to one arm. The ball can travel at speeds up to 150 miles per hour or more.

National Averages Comparison

T he United States is a federal republic, consisting of fifty states and the District of Columbia. Alaska and Hawai'i are the only non-contiguous, or non-touching, states in the nation. Today, the United States of America is the third-largest country in the world in population. The United States Census Bureau takes a census, or count of all the people, every ten years. It also regularly collects other kinds of data about the population and the economy. How does Florida compare to the national average?

Comparison Chart

United States 2010 Census Data *	USA	Florida
Admission to Union	NA	March 3, 1845
Land Area (in square miles)	3,537,438.44	53,926.82
Population Total	308,745,538	18,801,310
Population Density (people per square mile)	87.28	348.64
Population Percentage Change (April 1, 2000, to April 1, 2010)	9.7%	17.6%
White Persons (percent)	72.4%	75.0%
Black Persons (percent)	12.6%	16.0%
American Indian and Alaska Native Persons (percent)	0.9%	0.4%
Asian Persons (percent)	4.8%	2.4%
Native Hawaiian and Other Pacific Islander Persons (percent)	0.2%	0.1%
Some Other Race (percent)	6.2%	3.6%
Persons Reporting Two or More Races (percent)	2.9%	2.5%
Persons of Hispanic or Latino Origin (percent)	16.3%	22.5%
Not of Hispanic or Latino Origin (percent)	83.7%	77.5%
Median Household Income	$52,029	$47,802
Percentage of People Age 25 or Over Who Have Graduated from High School	80.4%	79.9%

*All figures are based on the 2010 United States Census, with the exception of the last two items.

How to Improve My Community

Strong communities make strong states. Think about what features are important in your community. What do you value? Education? Health? Forests? Safety? Beautiful spaces? Government works to help citizens create ideal living conditions that are fair to all by providing services in communities. Consider what changes you could make in your community. How would they improve your state as a whole? Using this concept web as a guide, write a report that outlines the features you think are most important in your community and what improvements could be made. A strong state needs strong communities.

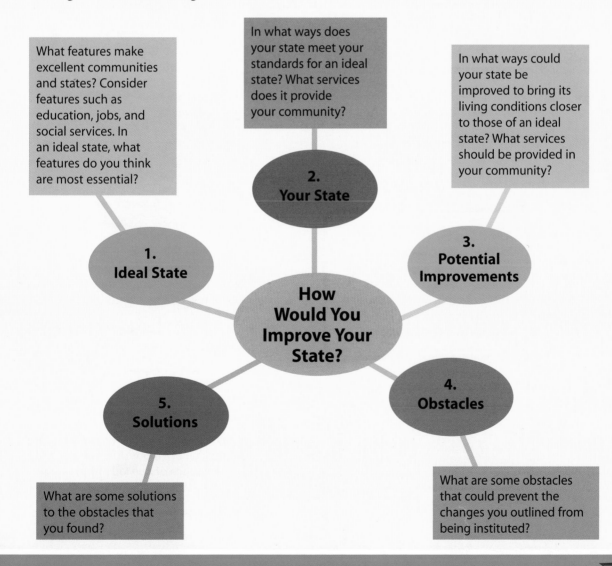

What features make excellent communities and states? Consider features such as education, jobs, and social services. In an ideal state, what features do you think are most essential?

In what ways does your state meet your standards for an ideal state? What services does it provide your community?

In what ways could your state be improved to bring its living conditions closer to those of an ideal state? What services should be provided in your community?

**2.
Your State**

**3.
Potential
Improvements**

**1.
Ideal State**

**How
Would You
Improve Your
State?**

**5.
Solutions**

**4.
Obstacles**

What are some solutions to the obstacles that you found?

What are some obstacles that could prevent the changes you outlined from being instituted?

Exercise Your Mind!

Think about these questions and then use your research skills to find the answers and learn more fascinating facts about Florida. A teacher, librarian, or parent may be able to help you locate the best sources to use in your research.

1 I am a big, pale brown cat with a long tail. People rarely see me, but I live in the forests of Florida and hunt deer. What am I?

2 What is the longest river in Florida?

3 I love to prowl through lakes, swamps, and canals and sun myself on warm logs or sunny banks. I may grow up to 15 feet in length, but I am usually smaller than another Florida animal I resemble. What am I?

4 Which wading bird has eyes that point downward so it can spot fish more easily?

5 Approximately how many islands bigger than 10 acres are found in Florida?

6 What is the oldest ongoing European settlement in the United States?

7 Which two fruits are crossed to make Florida tangelos?

a. orange and tangerine
b. grapefruit and tangerine
c. grapefruit and orange
d. two different kinds of oranges

8 Who was the first astronaut to walk on the moon, following the launch of *Apollo 11* from Cape Canaveral?

Words to Know

chickee: a log-frame house with a thatch roof, traditionally used by the Seminole and Miccosukee

citrus: trees or fruits from trees including lemon, lime, orange, and grapefruit

commercial: related to business, or done to earn money

endangered species: a type of plant or animal that is in danger of dying out

extras: people hired, often for the day, to appear in the background of a film

fossilized: ancient and hardened in rock, as with the remains of ancient plants and animals

habitats: the places where particular kinds of animals and plants are known to live

indentured servants: people who contract to work for a specific amount of time in return for travel to a specific place and upkeep. They are different from slaves in that their time in service is limited.

migratory: describes animals that move from place to place to live, depending on the season

peninsula: a piece of land jutting out into a body of water and almost entirely surrounded by water

phosphate: a rock that was formed in deposits over millions of years by layers of fossilized bones and shells and is used to make fertilizer

plantation: large farm for growing and harvesting crops, usually by slaves

refugees: people who flee to a foreign country because they fear for their safety or seek a better life

sinkholes: hollow places where water collects

subtropical: a type of climate that is nearly tropical, which is very hot and humid

wetlands: areas of land that are wet or swampy

Index

Log on to www.av2books.com

AV² by Weigl brings you media enhanced books that support active learning. Go to www.av2books.com, and enter the special code found on page 2 of this book. You will gain access to enriched and enhanced content that supplements and complements this book. Content includes video, audio, web links, quizzes, a slide show, and activities.

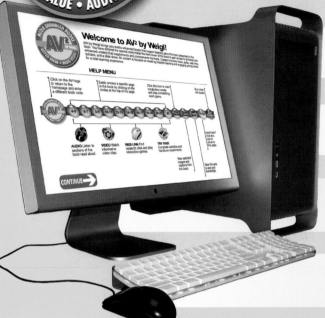

Audio
Listen to sections of the book read aloud.

Video
Watch informative video clips.

Embedded Weblinks
Gain additional information for research.

Try This!
Complete activities and hands-on experiments.

WHAT'S ONLINE?

Try This!	Embedded Weblinks	Video	**EXTRA FEATURES**
Test your knowledge of the state in a mapping activity.	Discover more attractions in Florida.	Watch a video introduction to Florida.	**Audio** Listen to sections of the book read aloud.
Find out more about precipitation in your city.	Learn more about the history of the state.	Watch a video about the features of the state.	
Plan what attractions you would like to visit in the state.	Learn the full lyrics of the state song.		**Key Words** Study vocabulary, and complete a matching word activity.
Learn more about the early natural resources of the state.			**Slide Show** View images and captions, and prepare a presentation.
Write a biography about a notable resident of Florida.			
Complete an educational census activity.			**Quizzes** Test your knowledge.

AV² was built to bridge the gap between print and digital. We encourage you to tell us what you like and what you want to see in the future.

Sign up to be an AV² Ambassador at www.av2books.com/ambassador.